NASCAR

THOMAS S. OWENS
DIANA STAR HELMER

TWENTY-FIRST CENTURY BOOKS
BROOKFIELD, CONNECTICUT

For Laura, Katherine, Thomas, David, and Rebecca, our nieces and nephews, and their dad, Thomas Jeffrey Helmer, who gave them their love of all things automotive.

Cover photograph courtesy of © Duomo

Photographs courtesy of Duomo: pp. 6 (left©1967; right©1998); SportsChrome USA/© Greg Crisp: pp. 9, 12, 25, 31, 33, 45 (both); © International Speedway Corp.: p. 10; Allsport: pp. 14 (©David Taylor), 15 (© Jon Ferrey), 42 (© David Taylor); AP/Wide World Photos: pp. 19, 27, 55; © Nigel Kinrade: pp. 21, 22, 35, 38, 40, 47, 52; SportsChrome East/West: p. 30

Library of Congress Cataloging-in-Publication Data
Owens, Tom, 1960–
    Nascar / by Thomas S. Owens and Diana Star Helmer.
    p. cm.
    Includes bibliographical references (p.) and index.
    Summary: Describes the fifty-year history of stock car racing, from its origins
at Daytona International Speedway in Florida in 1947 to current competitions among
such drivers as Jeff Gordon, Dale Jarrett, and Dale Earnhardt.
    ISBN 0-7613-1374-5 (lib. bdg.)
    1. Stock car racing—United States—Juvenile literature.
2. NASCAR (Association)—Juvenile literature. [1. Stock car racing. 2. NASCAR (Association)]
I. Helmer, Diana Star, 1962– . II. Title. III. Series: Owens, Tom, 1960– Game plan.
GV1029.9.S74094 2000
796.72'0973—dc21   99-10859   CIP
                                                                   AC

Published by Twenty-First Century Books
A Division of The Millbrook Press, Inc.
2 Old New Milford Road
Brookfield, Connecticut 06804

www.millbrookpress.com

CONTENTS

DAYBREAK IN DAYTONA

Each February, much of America is gripped by winter cold. But summer can only be chased so far. Summer stands its ground in Daytona, Florida, where a legendary racetrack promises an afternoon of red-hot sights, sounds, and struggles. Welcome to the Daytona 500.

Daytona is the birthplace of big-league auto racing. In December 1947, Bill France dreamed up the National Association for Stock Car Automobile Racing. ("Automobile" was later dropped from the full title.) To fans more than a half-century later, only six of those letters matter—NASCAR.

The 2.5-mile Daytona International Speedway has stood since 1959. The track is the launching pad for NASCAR excitement. Fans call the Daytona 500 their "super bowl," even though the race opens a season, instead of closing it. That's because, like a year-end championship, the Daytona 500 is a yardstick used to measure racing's masters.

Dale Earnhardt knew how important the race was. The pilot of the number 3 car had won 70 races going into 1998. He had also won seven season-points championships since becoming Rookie of the Year in 1979, a career feat matched only by Richard Petty. The only doubts about Earnhardt's skill were heard at season beginnings.

He had never won a Daytona 500.

Mario Andretti's car (left) in the 1967 Daytona 500 carried much less advertising than Dale Earnhardt's car (right) in the 1998 race. Sponsors provide extensive backing for modern racing teams.

ALWAYS THE FAVORITE?

Yes, Earnhardt won a qualifying race at Daytona for eight years running—1990 through 1997—but he had never won the main event. Two different years, he had led the race going into the last lap. Other times he had dueled the leader to the finish line. But the 200th lap always seemed to find Earnhardt just one eye-blink behind. And what went into the record books was not how close Earnhardt came year after year, but how he had lost this race 19 heartbreaking times. Was "The Man in Black," nicknamed for both his car and uniform, doomed for a career as the race's yearly uncrowned favorite?

The black cloud finally looked ready to lift at the 1997 Daytona 500. Now Dale Earnhardt had a new crew chief, Larry McReynolds. Before joining Earnhardt,

> . . . .
> **"You win some. You lose some. You wreck some."**
> —*NASCAR's seven-time champion Dale Earnhardt*

McReynolds had a hand in 22 wins. With the Robert Yates team, he had prepared cars for rising star Davey Allison. McReynolds won "all pro" honors from 1991 to 1995 for his crew-chief leadership. With McReynolds and Earnhardt together, the Goodwrench-sponsored car of Richard Childress Racing was fielding a dream team.

Earnhardt's fans believed that McReynolds would restore Earnhardt to his previous greatness, the 1994 points

How did Earnhardt's historic Daytona 500 win stack up against the record holders? In 1987, Bill Elliott qualified at 210.364 mph. In 1980, Bobby Allison's win came at a lap average of 173.473 mph.

championship. And sure enough, the 46-year-old driver logged 1997's fastest Daytona lap at 189.426 miles per hour. But as the race continued, Earnhardt's pit stops put him farther and farther back. When a backstretch accident finally took out his car for good, word got out that the new crew chief was using substitutes.

Substitutes? For this important race?

"We made the call on race morning that we would not let guys go over the wall because of some things that went on the night before," McReynolds explained to reporters. In other words, crew members may have been out late having fun and breaking team rules instead of thinking about Sunday's big race.

The season would get even stranger. Earnhardt's first year with McReynolds, 1997, became his first winless season in 16 years.

TURNING THE CORNER

But the next year looked like the good old days again. During the second qualifying race the Thursday before the 1998 Daytona, Earnhardt showed how he earned the nickname "The Intimidator." From lap 17 on in the 50-lap "Gatorade 125," Earnhardt led without serious challenges. His qualifying lap on the 2.5-mile course clocked at 191.006 miles per hour, putting Earnhardt's car fourth from the front in Sunday's starting grid. The qualifier victory meant that Earnhardt had won 30 different events at Daytona during his long career. But none of them ended with the numeral 500.

The famous race was having its 40th running in 1998. Earnhardt had been in half of them—this was his 20th try. No incidents marred the first half of the race, not until the first yellow caution flag dropped on lap 125. The slowed race gave time for all the contenders to pit their cars. Five laps later, the restarted battle turned into a 31-car trail of leaders. Earnhardt seized a lead, followed closely by six other drivers.

The cars of John Andretti and Robert Pressley tangled on lap 173, drawing another caution. Knowing this was the final pit stop, Earnhardt and his closest rivals all stopped for a right-side-only tire change and gas. The lead had changed hands 13 times during the 500. Earnhardt had controlled the lead 5 times. Now, with the Goodwrench pit crew working like lightning, Earnhardt returned to the track still in first place.

> **As the son of star NASCAR driver Ralph Earnhardt, Dale wanted the same job as his dad. To devote himself full-time to racing, Dale dropped out of high school. He still tells everyone his decision was "a damn fool thing to do."**

Earnhardt's years of experience created a masterful game plan in the final lap. The race seemed too close to call on lap 199 when Andretti and Lake Speed spun their cars, causing the final caution flag. Tailed by drivers Bobby Labonte and Jeremy Mayfield, Earnhardt found an odd assistant: Rick Mast, who had fallen more than a lap behind. Earnhardt used Mast's slower car as a screen to block Labonte and Mayfield. Labonte, who had won the "pole position" honor of starting in first place with his top qualifying time, finished second. Earnhardt had finally earned his Daytona triumph.

Pit road became a rainbow of uniforms awaiting the winner. A line of emotional members from every competing team wanted a look at the man from Kannapolis, North Carolina. Not just crew members but drivers, too. Once Earnhardt took an extra "victory lap" to celebrate and salute the crowd of more than 185,000 fans, he found getting his car to the winner's circle slow going. Everyone wanted in on the hand-slapping, as

Dale Earnhardt is overjoyed with his 1998 Daytona 500 win.

Earnhardt provided high fives by the dozen. Others just wanted to bang their congratulations on the sheet metal of the black number 3 car.

Even the Speedway's infield grass celebrated Earnhardt's victory. The delighted driver had spun his car to cut two "donuts" on the green, carving out the number 3.

The next day, Earnhardt told fans at a question-and-answer session of his winning game plan, his racing recipe for success. He explained that a penny glued to his dashboard for this race had come from a 5-year-old girl named Wessa Miller. The Make-A-Wish Foundation brought the wheelchair-bound Wessa from Washington State to see the race and meet her favorite driver.

The day before the 500, she gave Earnhardt the special coin.

Dale Earnhardt had a special good-luck penny glued to his dashboard for the 1998 Daytona 500 race.

"She said, 'I rubbed this lucky penny, and it's going to win you the Daytona 500. It's your race,' " he remembered.

"Inspiration is what it's all about," he said.

GETTING A "RIDE" 2

Where do NASCAR's drivers come from?

For drivers like Kyle or Adam Petty, being the children of known drivers has made them seem "born to race." But many drivers wait years for their "ride"—the job of driving for a team.

Drivers for Winston Cup teams must be 16 years or older. Kyle Petty was 18 when he landed his first ride for his father's team in 1979. Luckily, there is no maximum age for drivers—Dick Trickle was 48 when he was named NASCAR Rookie of the Year in 1989. Trickle had won more than 1,200 races on Midwestern tracks before moving south to try Winston Cup action.

Drivers of any age need to pass a physical examination. They must prove their driving experience. But, oddly enough, drivers do not need to have a driver's license! Once a driver passes a NASCAR driving test, NASCAR officials decide if the new driver will drive a full schedule or a limited. He may be limited to "short" tracks like Virginia's half-mile Martinsville Speedway. More experienced drivers could be allowed mile-long tracks, like Delaware's Dover Downs International Speedway. As drivers progress in experience, they progress to the most challenging tracks.

Drivers are hired by team owners for their past records and for their racing knowledge. Often, drivers serve as an extra mechanic. Mark Martin, who drives number 6 for Roush Racing, says: "When I'm racing,

I use the sense of smell a lot with the engine. When you get into tuning an engine to the max, you do your share of burning pistons, and a lot of times, I'll smell that and catch it before it goes bad." Only a driver can tell the pit crew just how a car feels, or what repair or improvement the engine needs before or during a race.

DRAFTING A PLAN

A NASCAR winner isn't simply the best-tuned, accident-free car. A driver's game plan mat-

A typical racing engine is complicated but spotless when ready for a race.

ters, too. Drafting, tailing a leading car to cut down your wind resistance, is one key. Next is the grade of the track. When drivers talk about how a speedway is graded, they don't mean A through F. The curves are banked at different angles. Go high, or low? Where is the track the fastest? Finally, Cale Yarborough, the first driver ever to win three straight Winston Cup titles (1976, 1977, 1978), once said: "Never tell your racing plans. You might need to use them again."

Time and experience help a driver develop strategy. "I started Winston Cup racing in 1979," Dale Earnhardt has said. "I got beat a lot. But I also learned a lot." Most drivers need years to watch and learn before they win. For example, only two faces under age 30 stayed in the top 10 driver standings for most of

> For its 50th anniversary celebration in 1998, NASCAR issued a list of its 50 "Greatest Drivers" of all time. Eleven drivers were active that year, including:
> 1 Geoff Bodine
> 2 Dale Earnhardt
> 3 Bill Elliott
> 4 Jeff Gordon
> 5 Ernie Irvan
> 6 Dale Jarrett
> 7 Terry Labonte
> 8 Mark Martin
> 9 Ricky Rudd
> 10 Rusty Wallace
> 11 Darrell Waltrip

the 1998 season. But Jeremy Mayfield, at age 29, was far from new in Winston Cup competition. He entered the season with 110 career starts. And 26-year-old Jeff Gordon was a veteran, too: He had won his first national championship in quarter-midgets when he was 8 years old.

Jerry Nadeau was the youngest, most inexperienced newcomer to enter Winston Cup ranks full-time in 1998. The 27-year-old Connecticut native began the year with the new Elliott-Marino team (Dan Marino, Miami Dolphins quarterback). However, after wrecking a half-dozen cars, failing to qualify for two races, and finishing no better than 21st, Nadeau was fired. He caught on with Melling Racing, driving to end the year in the "Cartoon Network Wacky Racer." Running a car decorated with different animated characters for each race, plus being mentioned regularly on a major cable network, guaranteed that Nadeau wouldn't be a mystery man in his second Winston Cup season. The Cartoon team rehired him for a full season in 1999.

Jerry Nadeau continues to race his attention-getting "Cartoon Network Wacky Racer." Here he races at Daytona on February 10, 1999.

Some of the drivers looking for NASCAR rides are women. Shawna Robinson became Rookie of the Year in the 1988 Goody's Dash Series. But she left racing in 1995, partly to marry and have children, partly because of difficulty in attracting and keeping a sponsor. After a three-year retirement, Robinson started 1999 in the ARCA circuit.

Patty Moise has tasted success in Busch Grand National racing. BGN racing has been a big part of her life since 1986—she even married competing BGN driver Elton Sawyer in 1990.

HELLO? PICK ME!

Kenny Irwin, Jr. grabbed headlines when Ernie Irvan left the Robert Yates Texaco car seat. Irwin campaigned for Irvan's old job, grabbing Yates's attention with repeated phone calls.

In 1987, Dale Earnhardt took the Winston race at Charlotte Motor Speedway with a legendary "pass in the grass." He was bumped off the track and into the infield by Bill Elliott. Earnhardt never let off the gas pedal. He returned to the track— still in the lead—and won.

Owner Yates was famous for gambling on 26-year-old Davey Allison. Allison had become 1987's Rookie of the Year, earning a career 19 wins before dying in a 1993 helicopter crash. Yates took another chance with Irwin—and got another Rookie of the Year in 1998.

But drivers don't have lifetime deals with race teams. Unlike the multiyear contracts signed by athletes in other sports, drivers often sign flexible contracts allowing them to change teams (and jobs!) before the season ends. In fact, fans expect this yearly switch of drivers from team to team, calling the second half of NASCAR events "silly season."

Any NASCAR season can turn serious in an instant, on the track or off. Ricky Craven seemed to have the deal of his life when Gordon's team, Hendrick Motorsports, signed him to start the 1997 season. But Craven's life and career became sidetracked after slamming into a wall at Texas Motor Speedway in April 1997. A year later, only four races into 1998, Craven admitted that his recovery from the head injury wasn't complete: He still had some vision problems. Craven sat out the

Patty Moise, shown here at Daytona in February 1998, is one of several women racers on the circuit.

Any driver needs to know traffic signs. **NASCAR** signs are flags. While most fans know that the checkered flag waves first to signal a winner, then that the race is over, other flags have important meanings.

YELLOW: Caution! Slow down, keeping your position.

GREEN: Track is clear; start racing again.

RED: Stop now! An accident blocks the track.

BLACK: Go to the pits. (If a driver's car is smoking or troubled and he doesn't know, this flag comes out.)

BLUE WITH YELLOW STRIPE: Let others pass; move aside. (A car more than one lap behind will see this flag.)

WHITE: One lap left till the race is done.

next 12 races, as doctors identified his post-concussion syndrome. When he finally got back behind the wheel of the number 50 car, Craven didn't come close to winning in four more races. Craven left Hendrick Motorsports on August 11, with neither side saying whether Craven quit or was fired. Was he treated unfairly? Did the sponsor or owner push him to drive before he was well?

Sometimes, one driver's misfortune can bring a big chance to a prepared newcomer. When Bill Elliott's father died and Bill had to attend the funeral, Matt Kenseth made his Winston Cup debut as a substitute in the number 94 car at Dover Downs International Speedway in September 1998. Kenseth stunned everyone with a sixth-place finish. Suddenly, teams began sizing up Kenseth's future behind their own wheels.

Dave Marcis is a rare example of how a driver can make his own ride. Born on March 1, 1943 , the Wisconsin native has been the dictionary definition of an "independent" driver. He has financed his own team in years when corporate sponsor money was not available, becoming his own boss. He depends on "weekend warriors," volunteers who keep his pit crew running. Marcis's game plan is to do things his way. Broadcasters even comment on the way Marcis dresses: He has raced for 30 years wearing old wingtip shoes. Marcis doesn't see anything odd about it. "They keep my feet cool," he says.

Getting a ride. Keeping that ride. Those are the game plans of drivers at various stages of their careers. As Nadeau sees it, "Rookies are going to make mistakes—that's why they're rookies. You're not born to go Winston Cup racing. Even Gordon needed a year and a half to start winning."

3 OWNING UP

The driver behind the wheel is only one member of a team. The owner behind the team is the start of a winning game plan.

Money matters in NASCAR. Even the basics are costly. The Goodyear Racing Eagle, the only tire approved for Winston Cup racing, cost $353 in 1998—for a single tire! In most races, teams can use up a dozen or more *sets* of tires. When all the extra equipment and travel is counted, top teams budget at least $150,000 per race. That doesn't add employee salaries into the mix, either. No wonder a team owner's costs can far outnumber the profits, especially for a losing team.

But team owners can make money from a winning team, not only with race "purse" earnings but with sponsorships. A car's front, back, and sides can make money when advertising is posted there. The same goes for team members. From head to toe, they are often walking billboards, displaying the names of bill-paying companies. Also, souvenir sales put more dollars in a team owner's pockets every time a collector buys a T-shirt or a die-cast miniature car.

Team owners are from many backgrounds. But they all share a love of racing.

Some team owners are former racers. Richard Childress started racing in 1969, driving his own cars. "I had a one-car garage on the end of my house, and I built my car under a shade tree. I built it for $400, and had a racing budget of $1,000." Childress had his best season as a driver in 1980, winning $157,530. In 1978, Childress was a top-ten finisher 11 times, even getting a third place for one race.

He retired as a driver in 1981 only when young Earnhardt was available to take the driver's place on Childress's team. Six championships later, the owner and driver are a historic pair.

NASCAR Winston Cup Series car owners are an important part of any game plan. Owners Richard Childress (left) and Joe Gibbs (right) were photographed at a Daytona practice session in February 1996. Childress is a former racer. Gibbs, a former NFL coach, was inducted into the pro football Hall of Fame.

BE YOUR OWN BOSS

But with money—lots of it—on the line, team owners haven't always been known as "loving parents." When Ricky Rudd wanted to form his own team in 1994, he took corporate sponsor Tide with him. Needless to say, that upset Rudd's old team owner, Rick Hendrick. Losing Tide meant Hendrick didn't have the cash he had counted on. So Hendrick struck back. He knew owners, not drivers, kept rights to car numbers. If Rudd wanted his own team, he could leave "5" and find his own number. That's why Rudd fans had to start following the "10" car.

Any team owner would welcome a big company sponsor willing to give millions of bucks yearly. But sponsors can cause problems, too.

Rudd faced more criticism in 1998, not for his new team's lack of wins but for his sponsor's behavior.

A group called People for the Ethical Treatment of Animals (PETA) claimed that manufacturer Procter & Gamble tested Tide detergent through experiments on animals. PETA wanted to pressure the company to change.

PETA members followed Rudd from racetrack to racetrack, week to week. The protesters drove a car that looked like Rudd's, except they called it the "Died" car. Rudd only wanted a winning team—he wasn't involved in making detergent. However, taking Tide money made him a sure target for anyone unhappy with the company.

> Many owners like to take an active role in plotting game plans with their drivers. Owners like the Stavola Brothers and Richard Childress list themselves on team rosters as "strategists."

OWNERS ARE OUTSPOKEN

Team owners may have to deal with the unexpected, not only from sponsors but also from cars, drivers, even other NASCAR owners. Jack Roush, head of Roush Racing, owns the cars raced by Mark Martin and Jeff Burton. To protect his cars and drivers, Roush developed the roof flaps that pop up as a car in an accident begins to spin. The flaps change the air currents, keeping most cars from flipping.

But other examples of Roush's trouble-shooting didn't have such positive effects. In 1998, Roush thought that rival driver Jeff Gordon's New Hampshire win was "miraculous." In fact, on August 30, 1998, Roush told reporters that Gordon's DuPont car had an illegal chemical

Safety features can often influence the outcome of a race. The roof flaps shown here pop up when a car begins to spin. The change in airflow helps to keep the car from flipping.

on the tires to make them last longer. NASCAR seized Gordon's tires and tested them, but found no cheating.

The accused cheater, Hendrick Motorsports, marked its 15th full year in Winston Cup racing in 1998. The team earned its fourth straight season-points championship, a NASCAR record. Terry Labonte's 1996 championship was sandwiched between three titles by Gordon. Owner Rick Hendrick fielded three cars in 1998: Gordon's, Labonte's, and the number 50 Budweiser car. Rick and his brother John built their racing empire from wealth earned from a series of auto dealerships.

Team owners come from circles outside racing, too. In the 1980s driver Harry Gant's team was owned by actor Burt Reynolds and a movie producer friend. Miami Dolphins

Some owners had to shut down teams after 1998 due to lack of bill-paying sponsors. Meanwhile, Petty Enterprises and the number 43 car set records in 1998 by marking a 27th-straight year of sponsorship with STP.

quarterback Dan Marino has been a partner with driver Bill Elliott since 1998. Elliott kept driving the number 94 car he owned since 1995 despite his investment in another team's car. "What I'm trying to do is what everybody else is doing," Elliott told reporters. "It's getting so expensive to do this and make it work with just one car. To do what you're trying to build and the things you need to do, I feel you need the money for two deals because it enables you to share expenses between the two operations." Other owners branch out into other NASCAR series, such as Busch Grand National, regarded as a top minor league and a stepping-stone to Winston Cup action.

A team owner's background can make a world of financial difference. Retired National Football League coach Joe Gibbs formed his own team in 1991. Even without a championship, his Winston Cup team gained fans and dollars. Gibbs's first driver, Dale Jarrett, wore a different NFL team's colors and logo on his helmet every week.

Bill Elliott continues to drive his car number 94 even though he and partner Dan Marino are investors in another team.

Experience taught Gibbs to try to keep the same pit crew and shop workers. "We know it's a team, and that you win with people and not cars," Gibbs says. "We try to have the best benefits and the best incentive plans." That means when the Interstate Batteries car wins prize money, everyone gets some of the winnings.

Billy Standridge knows how much it means when a "boss" appreciates a worker's efforts. Standridge was a crew chief in 1996 for Triad Motorsports' number 78 Ford. Later, he became a replacement driver. The taste of life behind the wheel made Standridge want more—his way. In 1998 he put together his own race team, on a tiny budget. Reporters raved how the 44-year-old former auto parts dealer was building his car himself! To help pay bills, Standridge formed a fan club called "Fans Can Race." For a $59.95 fee, fans could feel like they were paying part of Standridge's ride. The club, not a huge company, occupied the ad space on the car's front hood.

With one car, two cars, or three cars, owners are the ones who must pull together enough money and talent to make a winner. That job needs a game plan all its own. Being a winning owner is almost as tough as winning behind the wheel.

> · · · · · · · · · · · · · · · · ·
>
> **"All we need is a sponsor."**
>
> —*LJ Racing owner Joe Falk, after his unsponsored car, driven by substitute driver Todd Bodine, finished fifth at the NAPA 500 in Atlanta to end 1998*

4 HAIL TO THE CHIEF

Crew chiefs make good drivers into great ones. After all, most great teams have a great coach. NASCAR teams are no exception.

A crew chief worries first about the car, then about its driver. Each race day the crew chief considers the weather forecast and the layout and rules of the track. Only then can the fine-tuning begin.

Different tracks have different rules. Races at Daytona and Talladega (Alabama) tracks require teams to run with carburetor restrictor plates. These aluminum squares with four drilled holes (costing about $1.25 each), fit atop the engine, restricting the amount of air an engine can take in. In turn, the car's horsepower is restricted. The key to understanding horsepower is in the *power*. The more horsepower, the faster an engine can speed a car along.

NASCAR's governors have feared that cars would go too fast and lose control, flying off the tracks and into crowds. Racing's ruling body also believes that all cars will be nearly equal in speed if kept under 200 miles per hour. And if that is true, then only the skills of each driver, crew chief, and pit crew can determine the outcome of a race.

Yet fans and race crews alike have felt that carburetor restrictor plates restrict too much. Gary Nelson, the Winston Cup director who oversees inspection of cars, said that he would approve different alterations to slow down engines at special-rules races. But team owners with limited budgets have been slow to spend money in researching and developing new technology. Such small teams have had difficulty competing against teams that can buy better equipment.

IS BIGGER BETTER?

Crew chiefs used to be the smartest, best mechanics on a team. These days, they are more like head coaches. Top teams like the DuPont "Rainbow Warriors" of Jeff Gordon's car number 24 carry pit-crew rosters nearly the size of a baseball team. For 1998, the team's list of race assignment jobs numbered 21. By contrast, newer teams may have a dozen or fewer staff members for race days.

Some crew chiefs run a crew like a team. Others want members to feel like a family. Either way, talented crew members may be lured by better-paying jobs elsewhere with richer teams. Jimmy Makar, chief of

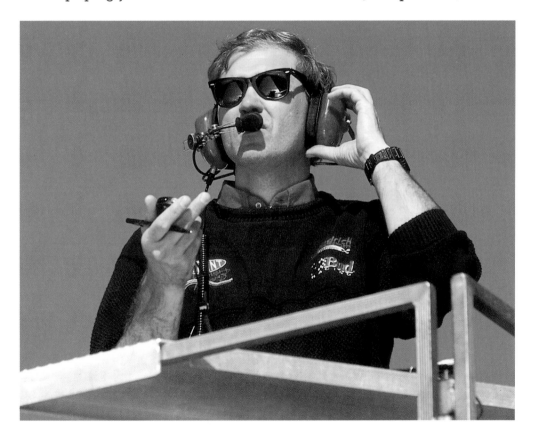

Former "Rainbow Warriors" crew chief Ray Evernham checks out a practice run.

> How can the driver talk to the crew chief on a two-way radio? The driver's radio button is rigged so he can activate it without letting go of the steering wheel.

the Bobby Labonte-driven number 18 car, told of his delight when his crew roster remained totally unchanged for a second season going into 1998.

Makar tried to pace his team to get through a long season. The crew chief himself averaged a 6:30 A.M. to 6 P.M. schedule at the shop on Mondays, Tuesdays, and Wednesdays. He would depart on Thursday for the next racetrack, returning home Sunday evening. NASCAR limits the hours that crew members can work each week before a race. This keeps crew members better rested and able to cope with a long season. But crew chiefs must relentlessly hunt for ways to get more work done in less time.

Can the job of crew chief be shared? The Wood Brothers racing team proved that two heads can be better than one with co-crew chiefs. Older brother Eddie Wood (born on April 8, 1952) is in charge of radio communications with his driver on race days. Little brother Len (born April 17, 1956) works as tire carrier on race days.

CREW CHIEF-IN-WAITING

A new role for crew chief is "consultant." When crew chief Steve Hmiel was released from Johnny Benson's team in 1998, he received a new job with a new title from the Dale Earnhardt team. He would build the crew for Dale Earnhardt, Jr.'s first Winston Cup team in 2000. After assembling and training the staff, Hmiel could assume the crew chief title and duties. Likewise, when owner Joe Gibbs started his team in 1991, he hired Jimmy Makar first, then asked Makar to assemble the rest of the crew talent.

Team-building knowledge often comes from having experience on a race team. Ryan Pemberton, who headed up the 1998 Skittles team with driver Ernie Irvan, got his start sweeping floors for owner Jack Roush and driver Mark Martin in 1988. By 1991 Pemberton was a team mechanic.

Racing teams see a crew chief like a coach. And coaches in such sports as baseball, basketball, football, and hockey have found that when the team is losing, leaders most often get the blame—and lose their jobs. But chances are you'll see that same man in another team's uniform, maybe before the end of the season. By October 1998, one in three Winston Cup teams had changed crew chiefs during the season. Teams that want to win today won't gamble on untested crew chiefs. Anyone who knows the ins and outs of the NASCAR scene is likely to get more than one chance at coaching a team to a championship, regardless of past records.

Estimates of pay for crew chiefs vary. The smallest teams start the job at about $75,000. While the top pay is about $500,000 yearly, most

Ray Evernham stressed teamwork and put together a pit crew that was fast and efficient. Here they service Jeff Gordon's car.

make between $175,000 and $225,000. Why so much? Crew chiefs can find painful challenges in their jobs. While leading the Wally Dallenbach-driven number 50 car, chief Tony Furr fell off the pit wall during a pit stop at a Daytona Beach night race. While atop the wall, his legs became tangled in an air hose, and Furr didn't get to see his driver finish 30th. He was in the hospital getting a cast on his broken leg.

Despite the danger in the pits, some crew chiefs still want to be in the middle of the action. Robert Larkins, crew chief for the number 4 Kodak car, did double duty as a jackman in 1998. A few other chiefs helped their drivers with tire changing. Still, more chiefs want to be free to coach team members, giving advice where needed.

A crew chief's game plan can make or break a driver. If you have doubts, just look at the qualifying times during a race. At 200 miles per hour, any car could travel the distance of a football field in less than one second. Passing another driver on the track might help a car improve its position—but only slightly. Drivers find that they can get ahead of a handful of foes with a quicker entry and exit from the pits.

The seven crew members over the wall for pit stops wear radio headsets because race noise makes it impossible to shout directions. Mostly, only the driver, crew chief, and spotter will talk on radio. Crew members will only answer questions.

That's why today's sponsors are selling their cars as team efforts. Crew chiefs are appearing with their drivers in television commercials. No longer do fans believe that drivers are the only force in winning game plans—NASCAR teams depend on dynamic duos.

PIT CREW PERFECTION

5

Pit crew members keep race cars running—faster and longer than last year, last month, last week. As they coax top performances out of their four-wheeled speed machines, pit crew members need to work as a machine themselves.

Every second matters during a race. That's why jobs are divided into single responsibilities. Instead of trying to remember many small but crucial tasks, a worker can focus on doing just one job as quickly as possible. Credit this idea to the Wood Brothers, who studied pit crew times in 1960. At that time, the average team took more than 45 seconds for gas and a tire change. By giving job assignments and planning where each crew member stood and when, the Wood Brothers created a dance routine of sorts—and pit stops under 25 seconds.

Of course, an important part of such pioneering is finding the best tools for crew members. Once, tires were changed with huge wrenches, all by hand. Air-powered wrenches make life easier and faster for crews, as do modern, hydraulic jacks.

Today's NASCAR rules allow only seven pit crew members over the wall on the track at one time. Rules sometimes change during the last stages of a race, when an eighth crew member may be used to wash the windshield, or see whether the driver needs a towel or other help.

A typical lineup of pit crews and their equipment

POLE POSITION

However, for most of the race, a driver doesn't get up-close service. A drink may be passed to him across the wall, using a long pole to maintain the "seven members only" rule. The windshield and front grille (which may get clogged with rubber and debris, stopping air flow into the engine) will be cleaned in the same way. Crews are always looking for a second-saving innovation. Some teams cover the windshield with a clear adhesive sheet, like contact paper. When the windshield is dirty, they just peel off the dirty layer.

Every pit crew job is important. The "sign board" member begins the pit stop. He signals the driver the proper location of the team's pit-box space. Based on qualifying speeds, drivers get to pick where on the track they will pit. A driver has to watch for traffic—including traffic from other pits—as he leaves the track and enters pit road. Tracks apply pit-road speed limits for safety. Exceed the speed limit, and the driver gets a "stop and go" penalty. The car must pit on the next lap and come to a complete stop. A team could also get a penalty for not having the car totally within the proper white-lined space. Pitting in another team's space breaks another rule. The car has to be moved before work resumes. NASCAR

This photograph clearly shows the white lines bordering the space allotted to a car and pit crew. Pits are carefully monitored by officials.

assigns at least one official to watch every two pits.

A team's car will sometimes be painted in special colors or a theme, telling about a new product of the sponsor's, such as a new movie. These flashy "paint schemes" don't last long. Often, the car is back to normal within a week. Collectors love buying miniature replicas of all variations of their favorite car.

Fans know that even the simplest-looking job is important. Every team member counts, which is why fans have adopted some team members as stars in their own right. Since 1981, Danny "Chocolate" Myers has been gas man for driver Dale Earnhardt, participating in six of his championships. Myers has been featured on a weekly radio program as well as on his own Web site. But hoisting two 11-gallon cans, each weighing about 80 pounds, isn't his only job. Good aiming and timing, getting as much in the car's gas tank spout as possible, is the gas man's goal. After all, more gas in the car means that the driver can go farther before needing another pit stop.

EVERY DRIP COUNTS

The partner of the gas man is the "catch can man." If a team doesn't clean up the runoff or spillage from a tank, the team is penalized by NASCAR. However, tidiness isn't the only reason for this job. Most important, the extra gas that doesn't get in the car's 22-gallon tank is measured. If the team can figure out just how much gas was needed to fill the tank, then the car's mileage can be calculated. Knowing how many laps a driver can run before the next pit stop can aid a winning game plan.

Many fans think that only drivers face danger during a race. Don't tell that to veteran crew members. Adam Petty, the son of Kyle and grandson of Richard Petty, drove in a Minnesota ASA (American Speed Association) race on September 7, 1998. ASA is a smaller league where future NASCAR drivers seek experience. Exiting from a late-race pit stop, the 18-year-old Petty didn't know what bump he hit. The bump

Each fuel can holds 11 gallons and is designed so the pit crew gas man can get as much in the car's gas tank as possible in a short time.

was crew chief Chris Bradley. He had crawled under the car to make an adjustment. No other crew members knew where Bradley was when the jackman lowered the car after the tire change, the signal for Petty to drive away fast. Bradley died that night.

> No hopping crew members allowed! Once, NASCAR didn't count a crew member with only one foot over the short wall. Those one-footed helpers would clean the windshield or car-front grille. Current safety rules don't allow such stretches. But today's longer, sturdier poles make it easier to comply with the rules.

For safety's sake, and to make every second count, teams work at making pit stops smoother than a well-planned dance. Former "Rainbow Warriors" crew chief Ray Evernham had his team practice three hours weekly before every race. Their 17-second pit stops were proof that practice can make near perfection.

But not every worker on a race-day pit crew spends the previous week at that team's workshop. The current team of driver-owner Dave Marcis features part-time helpers who only work on race day. Part-timers used to be the building blocks of all race teams. Nowadays, it's an old-fashioned idea used only by teams on a budget.

Debate began in 1998 over who the part-time crew members should be. To help speed up pit stops, some teams seemed to hire the best-conditioned athletes for crews. Was this unfair to poorer teams, whose mechanics might be more tired after a whole week's work?

The Lowes team pit crew answered that question when they won the World Pit Crew Championship in 1998. Before the October 31 race in Rockingham, North Carolina, 37 teams competed.

> One of the seldom-seen pit crew members is the gas runner. Because teams can keep just two fuel containers at a time, the gas runner must take empty gas cans back to track tanks to be refilled. Time counts here, too, because an empty car may be waiting.

The crews had to make a "full tires and gas" pit stop, just as in a race. The team from Richard Childress Racing logged 20.322 penalty-free seconds.

While the seven crew members wouldn't get rich from the total winnings of $30,200, the pit crew for the number 31 car had other reasons to celebrate. At the beginning of the next season, they would receive championship rings. And the team's hauler could carry the sign "1998 Union 76 World Pit Crew Champions."

Crew chief Larry McReynolds praised his winning crew. "I feel so bad that our sport is so one-person oriented. This isn't taking anything

Pit crews compete each year for the World Pit Crew Championship. The Lowes team won over 36 other teams to take the 1998 championship.

away from the drivers, but these guys that went across the wall today are not only the pit crew for this car, they're the ones that work 70- to 80-hour work weeks every week to get this race car to the race track," he said. "They're the ones that never get to carry their families [with them] and maybe get to see their kids once a week. That's the reason I'm so proud of them, for who they are and what they represent."

A WEEK TO WIN

6

Most teams have to race in order to make it to the race.

Many race teams have chartered or privately owned planes to transport them from Sunday to Sunday, track to track. But a team's actual route may not be from track to track, but from track to workshop to track.

More than half of NASCAR's teams are based in North Carolina. Their workshops are combinations of headquarters and hideouts. Teams sharing the same owner often have a common shop as a home base. For instance, Robert Yates Racing employs 85 people to run two Winston Cup teams. They all work in a center in Charlotte that measures about 70,000 square feet. By contrast, the Dave Marcis team gets by with a facility of 8,250 square feet in Asheville.

Monday is often an "off" day, a travel day for most teams. Business resumes on Tuesday. Under crew chief Ray Evernham in the 1990s, the "Rainbow Warriors" held morning meetings with shop workers, the engine and body specialists who try to field a car that will run faster and longer than before. Evernham called weekly Tuesday night meetings for the whole team. This was in addition to the 90-minute pit-stop practices on Tuesdays and Wednesdays. On Thursday afternoons, all key team members took the plane to the next race.

Teams have crews of engine builders in their workshops. All types of engines are created there. Some engines are designed for short oval tracks, some for twisting road courses. Teams may build a dozen

Engine builders really get into their work!

different engines per season. A special engine will be readied just for prerace qualifying, an engine that will give the most speed for just one lap. This engine is pulled before the race and replaced by another engine built to survive the stress of miles of laps.

GIVING CARS SKINS

Fabricators are metalworkers. They create the metal outer body around the frame of the car using a stock model, such as Ford Taurus, Chevrolet Monte Carlo, or Pontiac Grand Prix. Adjustments are made to decrease wind resistance and increase speed. Jimmy Makar, who would become crew chief for Bobby Labonte's number 18 car, started years earlier as a fabricator for another team. Like many beginners, he didn't make much money: less than $8,000 a year. But he learned about racing from the outside in.

The chassis specialist builds a car's insides, from shocks and springs on up. Evernham first made his name in NASCAR as a chassis specialist for Alan Kulwicki, who became the champion of 1992. A car's weight and handling depend on the chassis. Every ounce on the car is considered. Is the part needed, or would its weight slow the car down? The fuel gauge is an example. Since crew chiefs know how much gas can fit in the tank and can measure how much gas does *not* go in the tank at a pit stop, they can do the math. A fuel gauge is just extra baggage.

A driver may race only once a week. But a team's transport hauler driver may be on the road five days a week. Following a Sunday afternoon race, he'll have to race back to the East Coast workshop. If next week's race is in California, Arizona, or Nevada, the truck will need to leave the shop Monday, less than a day later.

Surprisingly, a driver may be the last person that a crew member sees before the race. Drivers may be traveling elsewhere, giving autograph sessions or making promotional appearances for sponsors. The year after Terry Labonte won his first championship in 1984, his sponsor asked him to make three appearances. After his 1996 championship in a car sponsored by Kellogg's, the cereal maker scheduled him for nearly 60 appearances.

But drivers do work with team members during testing sessions. Cars without all the paint and decals—but with the revised bodies, specialized engines, and fine tuning—will run without competitive pressure. Crew members can decide what a car needs to perform best at that track, or on similar speedways.

A service team metalworker makes a last-minute adjustment to a rear spoiler to fine-tune the wind flow.

FROM WIND TO WINS?

Wind tunnel visits are further between-race studies that can involve both driver and crew. A car's aerodynamics, its behavior in the wind, is studied. Building a car that moves as effortlessly as possible through gusts averaging 150 miles per hour is important. However, with costs averaging $1,500 an hour for a team's wind tunnel study, this research isn't done weekly. NASCAR used to allow teams to decide how much testing they would do. But owners with more than one team often have more money to spend on research. The best teams keep getting better, especially when an owner can pass information to all his drivers and crew chiefs. Today, NASCAR limits each team to 7 independent tests per year, 10 for teams with rookies. But before every race, time-limited practice sessions give all teams an equal chance to test tracks and machinery.

The team's hauler truck is packed tightly. Two cars (including a backup if the main car wrecks), spare engines, tools, and more are stuffed into the trailer. The cars are stored on platforms in the trailer top, leaving room for a kitchen and "living room" for crew members.

The teams make their first track appearances on Friday mornings. Competitors can see how other teams stand in season points by looking at how team haulers/transporters are parked. NASCAR allows last season's championship team to park first. The team currently first in points unloads second, with others following in order of points. Garage spaces are assigned in the same way.

Teams can compete in two rounds of qualifying, held on the Friday and Saturday before a race. Fans can buy tickets to these prerace days, at prices lower than race day admission. Practices may last up to two hours before qualifying starts, giving every team a chance to test the track and make adjustments to their machines. On Saturday of race weekend, a morning practice precedes more qualifying. Any team with a lap time ranked 26th or lower can try again in this second round.

Maybe the weather will be better. Maybe not. For better or for worse, only the second-round time will count.

After the second round, a final practice is held in the afternoon. Reporters have nicknamed this event "Happy Hour." Teams get 60 final minutes to get geared up for the race. Then NASCAR closes the team garages with an announcement at the same time every evening. No late, extra work is allowed.

For most Winston Cup races, the field allows only 43 cars. Anywhere from 45 to 50 teams may try to qualify, though. The result? Maybe a half-dozen cars that weren't among the fastest qualifiers just have to

Cars line up for a practice session at the Daytona 500 International Speedway before the race on February 10, 1998.

pack up and go home. Still, qualifying rounds make all cars equal for one lap. With a top time, last week's last-place driver can start the race first, winning pole position.

But speed only determines the first 36 starters. Cars that don't make the grade can still get one of four "provisional" spots given to drivers with the most points in the present season, currently ranked in the top 25. Two more spots will include the next-highest drivers. The final provisional, the 43rd spot, is saved for a previous Winston Cup champion who isn't in the field.

Between races, fans may see "show cars" on display around the country. These aren't just pretend copies of the cars of NASCAR drivers. These cars often are former race cars with records, now retired. When you see a show car, ask the team representative about the car's past.

Before the last race of the 1998 season, NASCAR announced important rules changes. One new rule allowed teams to make their car's rear spoiler bigger, giving cars more stability on corners and when passing. Jeff Gordon's team worked nonstop in the days before Atlanta's final race to use the changes to their advantage. Gordon said that, without the spoiler adjustments, he wouldn't have been able to take the lead in the final laps of the race.

Fans may think a race is won or lost in seconds. But those outcomes actually spring from days, weeks, and months of fine-tuning game plans.

7 RACE DAY RITUALS

Most often, Sunday is the big day.

Garages open at 6 A.M. The workshops were locked Saturday night to assure that no teams would put in extra, "illegal" work hours and get an unfair advantage.

The "pit wagons" or "war wagons," those huge toolboxes-on-wheels, are headed into the pit stalls. Replacement tires are arranged. Air-powered wrenches are tested, and the jack is oiled. The lug nuts for tires are glued on with a yellow adhesive. The airguns will break the glue seals when the tires need changing.

NASCAR gives all cars another race day inspection to guard against any illegal changes by teams, and to help increase safety. NASCAR rules say that teams must go through no fewer than three and no more than six inspections per weekend.

A meeting is required before each race day for all drivers and crew chiefs. NASCAR officials review rules, old and new, and discuss what to watch out for on this particular track. Drivers who don't go to the meeting could be penalized, made to start the race at the back of the pack.

A RACING CHURCH

A minister from Motor Racing Outreach (MRO) offers a prayer at each meeting. MRO holds a Sunday chapel service for team members and families, people who are unable to attend regular church because of work.

Teams are at full strength on Sunday mornings. To save money, some owners fly in certain crew members only for race day, then ship them back home the same night. That saves in employee pay, food, and overnight stays.

Meanwhile, the drivers are on their own to prepare for the race. Drivers will either be hidden away in the team hauler, or they may be in a private motor home, which they use to depart the track quickly after the race. They have decided carefully on what food to eat before driving—

Team haulers (top) enter the parking area. The photo (bottom) shows a line of parked haulers and some of the equipment they carry.

something, but not too much. Ricky Rudd has only a ham or turkey sandwich before the race. The hauler also doubles as a dressing room where drivers don their fireproof uniforms covered with sponsor logo patches.

Temperatures may be more than 50 degrees hotter inside a race car than outside during a race. That's why drivers drink plenty of liquids before driving. But almost all drivers insist that all that fluid doesn't result in a need for bathroom breaks. Supposedly, Kyle Petty once said, "You might think it could happen, but it never does." Drivers make their last bathroom trip before driver introductions.

Some fans object if they hear a TV or radio reporter say a car has a "blown motor." Motors run with electricity— no gas needed. So how could it blow up? All NASCAR vehicles have engines. Engines run on fuel. To be fair, the confusion may come from the companies that build Winston Cup teams' engines: the Ford Motor Company or General Motors! What's in a name?

The starting grid, the car-by-car lineup determined by previous speeds in qualifying runs, is set up in a quiet way: Teams *push* their cars to their assigned starting spots. That's why the traditional public-address announcer's cry of "Start Your Engines!" brings such excitement in the grandstands.

Before the race begins, each team checks its spotter, known as the "eye in the sky." Spotters climb to the highest spots available to watch the race, often atop the control tower at a track. Using a two-way radio, the spotter can relay what he or she sees both to the driver and crew chief. If a cloud of smoky dust awaits a driver round a curve, the spotter will relay news of where the crash is and how to avoid it.

RACING THE RAIN

Of course, accidents may not be the only delay in a race. The final race of the 1998 season seemed as if it might never end. Rain delays at the Atlanta Motor Speedway interrupted the November 8 race for a

Spotters check race conditions and relay the information to the drivers and crew chiefs.

combined seven-plus hours. Some teams used that time to work with the weather. Knowing that a late-starting race will often be cut down to fewer laps, teams retooled their engines to run a cooler, shorter race.

NASCAR races only on dry tracks because Winston Cup cars use tires with practically no tread. Tread gives a car better control in wet conditions. Smooth tires can grip more of the road, which gives superior control on dry roads but is dangerous on wet tracks. NASCAR will halt a race under even the gentlest rain, for safety's sake. A heating, vacuuming vehicle, similar to the Zamboni machines used on ice rinks, is used to try to dry the tracks on wet race days.

Fans at many tracks see the race from the inside out. Staying on the infield for the weekend, fans camp out in motor homes. Camping isn't free, but there's no better way to feel "in" the race.

Some drivers must wait a week to take a bow. At prerace ceremonies, drivers who won contingency awards from the past week will get honors and prize money. For instance, MCI would give $5,000 to the driver with the fastest lap time in each race. At season's end, MCI gave the driver with the fastest lap of the year $50,000. Even without winning a checkered flag, a driver can still win something.

During rain delays, some crew chiefs are busy with calculators. They continually study the complex rules for the points championship. The crew chiefs tell their drivers the minimum results needed to produce. More points can mean more award money at season's end. Meanwhile, a team scorer is studying how everyone else is doing in the race for points. Women in racing have often found jobs as scorers to be some of the most open to them.

In the winner's circle, the winner gladly tips his cap, or caps, to all his sponsors. A bottle of the sponsor's soda pop will mysteriously appear in the winner's hand—or on his car roof! Then the winner changes his cap, donning one with the name of another sponsor, then another and another, providing pictures that will be used in future ads. After all, those sponsor dollars did help the winner's team build a winning car.

OTHER HEROES

The winner gets the glory, the prize, and the applause. But sometimes the most heroic races are not run by the winner. Karen Huseonica, Internet webmaster for Ted Musgrave (www.tedmusgrave.com), says her favorite driver was a comeback star at the Food City 500 in Bristol, Tennessee, on March 29, 1998—a race he didn't win.

"Ted Musgrave started in 29th (after qualifying) and had to battle toward the front. And that's what he did until a wreck, which was no fault of his, cost him two laps while his pit crew repaired his car," she says.

"Back on the track, Ted worked the steering wheel and throttle with precision to get his two laps back. This meant passing all the cars twice. Ted's pit crew worked wonders and clocked some of the fastest pit stops for 4 tires and 22 gallons of gasoline—less than 18 seconds. On lap 341 (of 500 laps), Ted made his way into the top ten and never looked back."

How did Musgrave explain the amazing return? "Guts, determination, and a lot of skill on the crew's part for our good finish today," he said.

There are many different ways to win.

At race's end, NASCAR officals hold one last inspection. The car of the winner, pole-position winner, and second- and third-place drivers are usually singled out.

But it isn't over, not even after the winner is announced and the interviews are given. Getting out of the track, back on the road, and back to the workshop is the last step in the game plan. It takes more than one win to make a champion.

8 THE BIG RACE

"Fans Against Gordon!"

"Anyone But Gordon!"

Despite his youthful good looks and TV commercial fame, Jeff Gordon wasn't adored by all NASCAR followers. After 11 wins in the season, some fans of other drivers wanted the victories to be spread around. They booed and waved signs, showing their frustration.

The anti-Gordon fans had more bad news waiting at the 393-lap race in Rockingham, North Carolina, on November 1, 1998. Gordon's DuPont Chevrolet was sure to bring home another season-points championship, unless a huge disaster struck. He needed only a 40th place finish for enough points to secure the crown, which would be his second straight and third in four years. And this wasn't even the last race of the season!

Not since Dale Earnhardt's 1994 crown had a driver had the chance to settle the championship before a season's official end. Anti-Gordon critics worried that the 27-year-old would play it safe to survive the whole race, gaining the points needed for the huge championship payoff without racing full-out to the finish line. And evidence supported such complaints: Gordon had never won a November race in his Winston Cup career.

But ever since Gordon joined the Winston Cup ranks with Hendrick Motorsports in 1993, when he was named Rookie of the Year, he had maintained one game plan. "We don't think about championships. We just get ready for the next race," he said.

EIGHT MEN AHEAD

The native of Vallejo, California, qualified ninth to begin the race at Rockingham. Mark Martin, second to Gordon in points before the race, was the first-place starter, winning pole position with a qualifying time of 156.502 miles per hour, taking 23.394 seconds to complete a lap.

By lap 114, Gordon's number 24 car had passed Martin for fourth place. He worked his way to first place by lap 120. Gordon kept the lead by staying on the track when the other leading drivers pitted. "Really, most of the day I wasn't even thinking championship," Gordon told reporters. "[Crew chief] Ray [Evernham] came on the radio and congratulated me, because I wanted to know. I was excited, but at the same time it was like, 'Don't mess up my concentration.' I wanted to win the race."

When Jeff Gordon was 12, he wanted to race something besides go-carts. However, California had age restrictions on what kind of vehicles someone so young could race. Indiana had none. When he turned 13, his family moved so Jeff could began sprint car racing.

Likewise, Evernham stopped any mid-race celebration. He told the crew, "We still have a job to do."

Gordon faced his biggest challenge in lap 268, not from another driver but from his own team. During a pit stop tire change, a rear tire got loose from Gordon's car. After it rolled across pit road, NASCAR enforced a penalty. The car would be held in the pit for 15 seconds.

"Our guys never make that mistake. It never happens to them," Gordon said. But, he added, "Every once in a while you're going to slip, and something like that is going to happen." Did it matter? "It definitely put

Jeff Gordon's car in a pit stop at the race in Rockingham, North Carolina, on November 1, 1998. During this stop, one of his tires rolled across pit road, and NASCAR officials held the car in the pit for 15 seconds.

us way behind," Gordon confessed. "It was disappointing to be leading those guys and then come out a half-lap behind. I couldn't even see them."

A LAUGHING MATTER?

Evernham joked later that when he fetched the tire, he tried to pretend that it was someone else's. He pointed to the nearby pit of Jeff Burton's number 99 car as if to signal that he had their tire. But officials weren't fooled.

With only eight laps left, Gordon grabbed the lead from Rusty Wallace. "After the last restart, I was able to keep Rusty in my sights," he said. "When he went low in the turn, like he always seemed to do, I was able to go high to pass him." Seven years of Winston Cup competition had taught Gordon a veteran's game plan of studying the habits of other drivers.

In the final lap, Dale Jarrett offered one last challenge. If Gordon wanted to win, he was going to have to fight for it. By only 0.520 second, Gordon took the checkered flag. The entire race took 3 hours, 6 minutes, 44 seconds.

Third-place Wallace had led in all but three of the race's first 79 laps. What happened? "I wore the tires out," he told reporters. "I thought I had plenty to win the race, but once I saw Gordon coming, there was nothing I could do. I was more surprised to see my car fall off like it did. We missed a little bit on the spring and shock setup."

In all, 10 drivers shared 20 lead changes for the day. Gordon held the lead only three times, for a total of 28 laps. But they were the laps that counted most. Earnhardt, the Daytona 500 winner, had tasted victory for a few fleeting minutes near the race's end, leading for laps 270 through 277. In the end, he rolled in ninth, with an eighth in points standings at 3,804, while Gordon became the first driver ever to exceed 5,000 points in one year (5,143).

Jarrett's last-second showdown with Gordon amazed everyone who had followed the season of the AC Delco driver. From October 25 through 29, Jarrett was hospitalized with gallstones. Hut Stricklin had even driven warm-up laps that day, in case he would be needed to substitute for the ill driver. But Stricklin never got to drive a lap. Second-place Jarrett issued the highest praise for the winning team. "They win championships by winning races," he said. In other words, Gordon's title came fair and square.

After the checkered flag, the crew chief's first comments on the radio to his driver were short and sweet. "Congratulations. You know what month it is," Evernham said. No more 0-for-November talk. No talk of winning a points title the easy way. The "Rainbow Warriors" had won the war of words—at least for 1998.

Of course, the season wasn't finished, and neither was Gordon. One week later, in the final race of the season, Gordon beat second-place rival

Dale Jarrett by 0.739 second—and Gordon didn't stop there. He also tied Richard Petty's once-untouchable mark of 13 wins in a season. Also, for the second time in a single year, Gordon won the "No Bull 5" bonus of $1 million.

His team finished the season with more than $8 million in winnings and its third title in four years—a pot of gold at the end of the "Rainbow Warriors" game plan.

The "Rainbow Warriors" continued their winning game plan when Jeff Gordon beat Dale Earnhardt to the checkered flag to win the Daytona 500 on February 14, 1999. The team would need a new game plan to start the year 2000: In late 1999, crew chief Ray Evernham quit to pursue his dream of owning his own team.

GLOSSARY

apron   the flat, lower edge of the track, which allows drivers to come and go from the pits.

banking   the angle of sloping on a track, from outside wall to apron. The banking of some curves and corners may change a driver's game plan.

bite   a car's weight distribution. The bite on each wheel can be changed by turning the jacking screws.

blister   of tires, to get so hot that the outer rubber bubbles and strips off the wheel.

blown engine   a major engine failure, sure to eliminate a driver from a race.

Busch Grand National   considered a training league for future Winston Cup drivers. Sometimes written BGN.

caution flag   one of various flags used to communicate with drivers during a race. For example, the yellow flag means to slow down and be careful. Red means stop.

chassis   the frame of the car, where the sheet metal is placed.

DNF   "did not finish." Abbreviation for driver whose car was eliminated in midrace due to a wreck or engine trouble.

deck lid   trunk lid.

depth gauge   a pit stop tool placed in the tiny indentations on a tire. The gauge measures how much surface tread is left.

dialed in   said of a race car, prepared for top performance at a certain racetrack; a slang expression.

draft   a plan in which a driver tails a faster car. The second driver uses the first as a shield and windbreaker, saving fuel and wear on his car.

firesuit   the zippered jumpsuit worn by drivers, constructed of fire-resistant material to protect drivers from flames.

flat-out   racing at top speed.

fuel cell   a gas tank on a race car holding 22 gallons. A fuel cell is durable enough not to explode in a high-speed collision or crash.

groove   the portion of the track where the most cars have been running, making it the fastest place to travel. The groove changes as loose rubber from blown tires is mashed into the track surface.

handling   the way a car behaves on the track.

hauler   the semitruck-trailer rigs used to transport a team's cars and gear from racetrack to shop to racetrack. A hauler will bring two ready-to-race cars, one as a backup. The hauler also includes five engines, and the tools and supplies needed to fix any problems at the track.

horsepower   the measurement for judging the amount of power an engine creates.

infield   the grassy area inside the racetrack, where wrecked cars may wind up.

jackman   the pit crew member who runs the jack, used to raise and lower the car for tire changes.

loose   the term to describe how the back end of a car handles during a race. Too loose is too hard to control.

lug nut   the bolt that holds a wheel onto a car. An air-powered wrench is used to loosen and tighten lug nuts during pit stops.

marbles   driver slang to describe the chunks of rubber, rock, and other debris that land on the upper, higher area of the track. Driving over "marbles" isn't easy or good.

pace car   a car driven by a NASCAR official to lead, or pace, all cars around the track to start a race, or following caution periods, to ensure that all drivers begin at similar speeds.

pit a space assigned to a race team on pit road, where repairs and service must be performed during the race.

pit stop in the pit. Refueling, changing tires, realigning the car body and keeping the driver refreshed are typical pit stop duties. Only seven crew members at once are allowed to go over the wall into the pit area to perform car maintenance during the race.

polesitter a driver who has earned the fastest time in prerace qualifying heats, winning the right to start first, or on the pole.

push of a race car, meaning difficult to turn. Drivers struggle to get a "pushing" car around corners, worrying about wall crashes.

qualifying designating a run of one or more laps timed to judge the fastest car in the field. The first qualifying is often on the Friday afternoon before race day. A second qualifying happens on Saturdays. The slowest cars don't qualify to compete in the race.

restrictor plate a thin metal plate, placed between the carburetor and intake manifold, introduced by NASCAR in 1988. The plate lessens the air and fuel to the engine, reducing an engine's horsepower by about 300. Restrictor plates are currently required for racing at Daytona and Talladega.

ride slang for a driving job with a NASCAR team.

roll cage a protective cage of tubes, 1.75 inches thick, built to protect the driver during a crash or accident in which the car rolls onto its roof.

roof flaps roof-mounted panels of thin metal. Roof flaps interrupt air currents that could flip a car during out-of-control spins. Without roof flaps, more cars would flip through the air during accidents.

scuffs used tires. Some teams purposely scuff tires for future use, knowing that a car responds best with used tires.

setup how a team adjusts a car's shocks, springs and overall chassis to respond best to a particular track.

short track a racetrack less than 1 mile in length.

souvenir trailer a team truck at a racetrack, which sells collectibles and clothing bearing the team and driver name, number, and likenesses.

speedway a racetrack a mile or more in distance.

spoiler the metal fin extending across the rear deck lid of a car. The spoiler reduces wind resistance, increasing speed.

sponsor business or company that supports a race team with money. The sponsor's name and logo will appear on the car, and on all driver and team member clothing.

spotter a team member who watches the race from the grandstands, connected by two-way radio to the driver and crew chief. The spotter warns the driver about upcoming track situations, including accidents and positions of other cars. The spotter tells the crew when the car enters pit road for a pit stop.

tear-off a clear sheet applied to a car windshield, removed halfway through a race as a way of cleaning the glass.

tight of a car, difficult to turn into corners.

wall 1. the structure bordering the racetrack. 2. the safety wall that separates the pit crew from pit road. Crew members go over the wall to service the car during a pit stop.

webmaster a person who creates and maintains an Internet Web site by gathering, writing, and editing information.

wedge to turn a screw to change pressure on a car's rear springs, altering the way it handles.

Winston Cup the highest level of NASCAR racing competition.

FOR MORE INFORMATION

Books

Brinster, Dick. *Race Car Legends: Jeff Gordon*. Philadelphia: Chelsea House Publishing, 1997.

Mello, Tara Baukus. *The Pit Crew*. Philadelphia: Chelsea House Publishing, 1999.

Books for Older Readers

Alexander, Don. *Think to Win: The New Approach to Fast Driving*. Cambridge, Mass.: Robert Bentley Publishers, 1995.

Freeman, Criswell, ed. *The Book of Stock Car Wisdom*. Nashville: Walnut Grove Press, 1996.

Huff, Richard. *The Insider's Guide to Stock Car Racing*. Chicago: Bonus Books, 1997.

The Official NASCAR Handbook. New York: HarperHorizon Books, 1998.

Internet Resourses

www.nascar.com
The official site sponsored by NASCAR.

www.jeffgordon.com
Gordon's official site. He was one of the first drivers to launch his own space on the web.

www.crewchiefclub.com
Some of racing's top crew chiefs have combined to provide fans with more understanding and appreciation of the job.

www.webracers.com
A classy fan-produced page, focusing on Busch Grand National racing. Next season's Winston Cup stars could be BGN headlines now.

www.jayski.com
Can a fan be a great detective? Check out this information-stuffed "Silly Season Site," and discover the truth and rumors of upcoming team changes.

http://members.aol.com/nascarryan/nascarfamily.html
Called "NASCAR Family Chat," here's a fine address collection of nearly every type of NASCAR site imaginable!

INDEX